LAURA LYNNE

Living In His Dreams

AuthorHouse™
1663 Liberty Drive
Bloomington, IN 47403
www.authorhouse.com
Phone: 833-262-8899

Because of the dynamic nature of the Internet, any web addresses or links contained in this book may have changed
since publication and may no longer be valid. The views expressed in this work are solely those of the author and do not
necessarily reflect the views of the publisher, and the publisher hereby disclaims any responsibility for them.

Any people depicted in stock imagery provided by Getty Images are models,
and such images are being used for illustrative purposes only.
Certain stock imagery © Getty Images.

This book is printed on acid-free paper.

ISBN: 978-1-6655-5873-0 (sc)
ISBN: 978-1-6655-5875-4 (hc)
ISBN: 978-1-6655-5874-7 (e)

Library of Congress Control Number: 2022908264

Print information available on the last page.

Published by AuthorHouse 06/14/2022

authorHOUSE®

Foreword

Zachary "Zach" Lars was born on December 9, 2001. His parents, Eric and Joni, were thrilled to bring their beautiful baby boy home to his four older siblings. After a full-term pregnancy, all showed that Zach was just perfect, healthy. But by the age of 2, Zach began showing signs of delay, speech difficulties, and behavior issues.

Doctor visits and testing resulted in several misdiagnoses. It was not until Zach was admitted to the Emergency Department with prolonged seizing that the medical community started to question and reevaluate. Zach's seizure activity was out of control, and the emergency physicians tried various epilepsy medications before being able to effectively calm his symptoms.

Zach's team of physicians continued to monitor his progress. And, eventually, upon performing genetic testing, the diagnosis of Dravet Syndrome was confirmed; Zach was 5 years old. Efforts to reduce the number of seizures and lessen their intensity have, unfortunately, been ongoing ever since. At one point, when Zach was 7, his seizures worsened to such a degree that he became mute. His mutism, neurologically-based, remained for a 9-month period.

There is no cure for Dravet Syndrome. Those with this rare form of epilepsy often have movement disorders that make normal tasks like walking, balancing, eating, and communicating difficult. In Zach's particular case, he also has profound cognitive impairment. Though he is now 20 years old, he functions socially and intellectually at the level of a 2-3-year-old.

Zach's mother, Joni, worked tirelessly to provide Zach with all the help and care he needed. She loved him beyond measure. Sadly, Joni passed away in a bicycle-car accident in June of 2016. This book was written in her memory, a way of honoring her place in the world. She was a wonderful, loving mother of 5 children. They are her legacy.

Zach was 20 years old. But Zach did things differently from other boys his age.

Zach walked
differently.

He ate differently.

He talked differently.

Sometimes it was hard to understand what Zach was saying, but that didn't stop Zach. He would try and try until others could understand.

Zach also listened differently. When his mind was full of this:

Zach loved music, baseball,
and playing with friends,
yet, most of all, Zach loved
everything about fire trucks
and fire rescue.

He would play dress-up and wear
a fire coat and fireman's hat.

10

His dad would help him drive fancy golf carts that looked like fire trucks, ones with flashing lights and loud sirens.

Zach had a kind of
epilepsy called Dravet
(druh vay) Syndrome.
This made Zach special.

And while he needed help to do most things like take a bath, get dressed, and fix breakfast, Zach could still do one thing all by himself. He could dream.....

In his dreams, Zach could be the
town superhero, jumping down
fire poles and racing to fires in his
hook-and-ladder truck.

He could hold the hose steady as water shot out and blasted the flames.

15

In his dreams, Zach could
do everything, be anything.
He was free.

Printed in the United States
by Baker & Taylor Publisher Services